FOUR POINTS
ool of Tourism
QUEEN
RHAPSODY
Metro
Metro
Metro
Sorry...Not in S
Metro

PHILLIPS FOX
PHYSICAL

ACCOUNTING LEGAL
CONSULTING ACCOUNTING

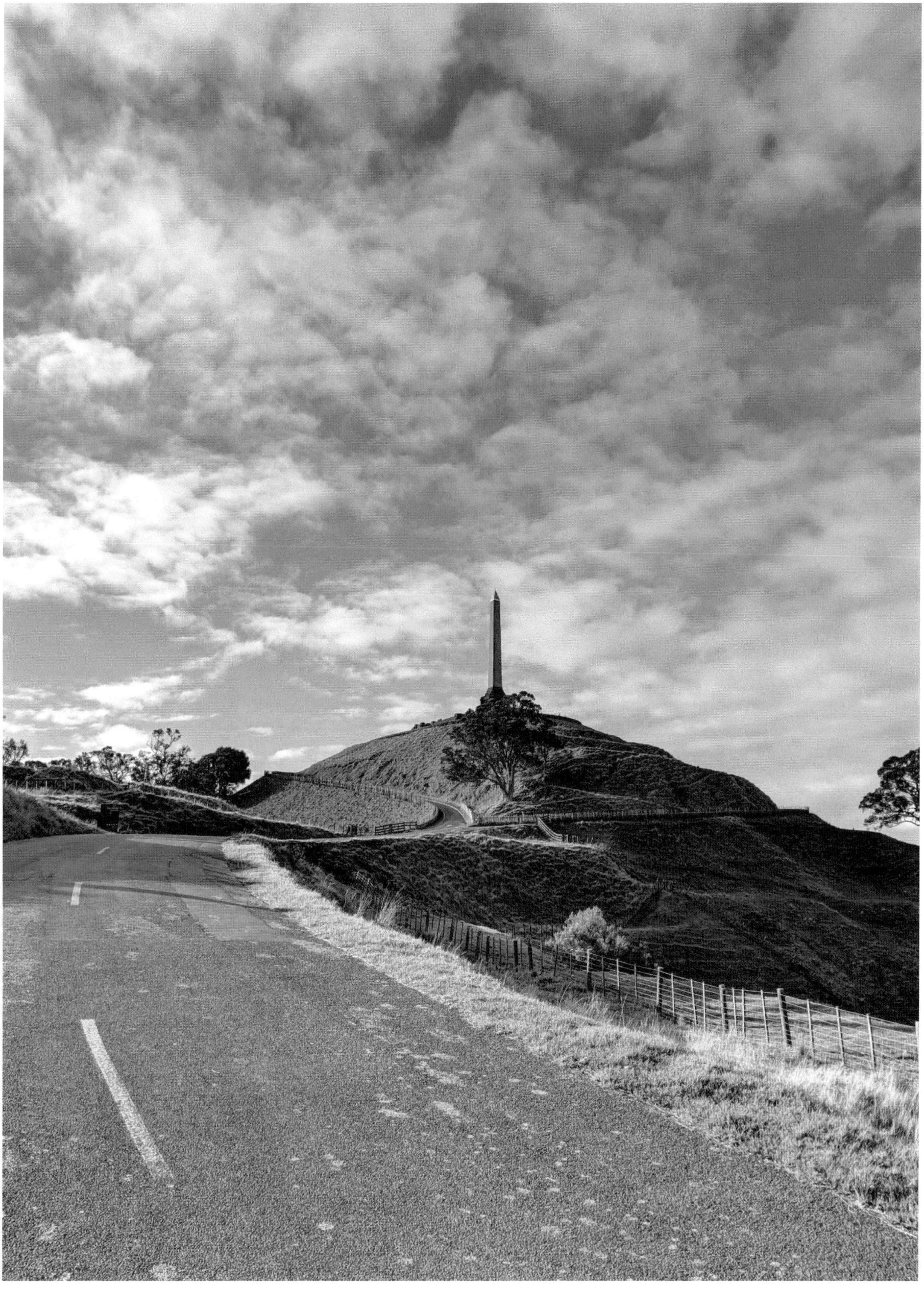

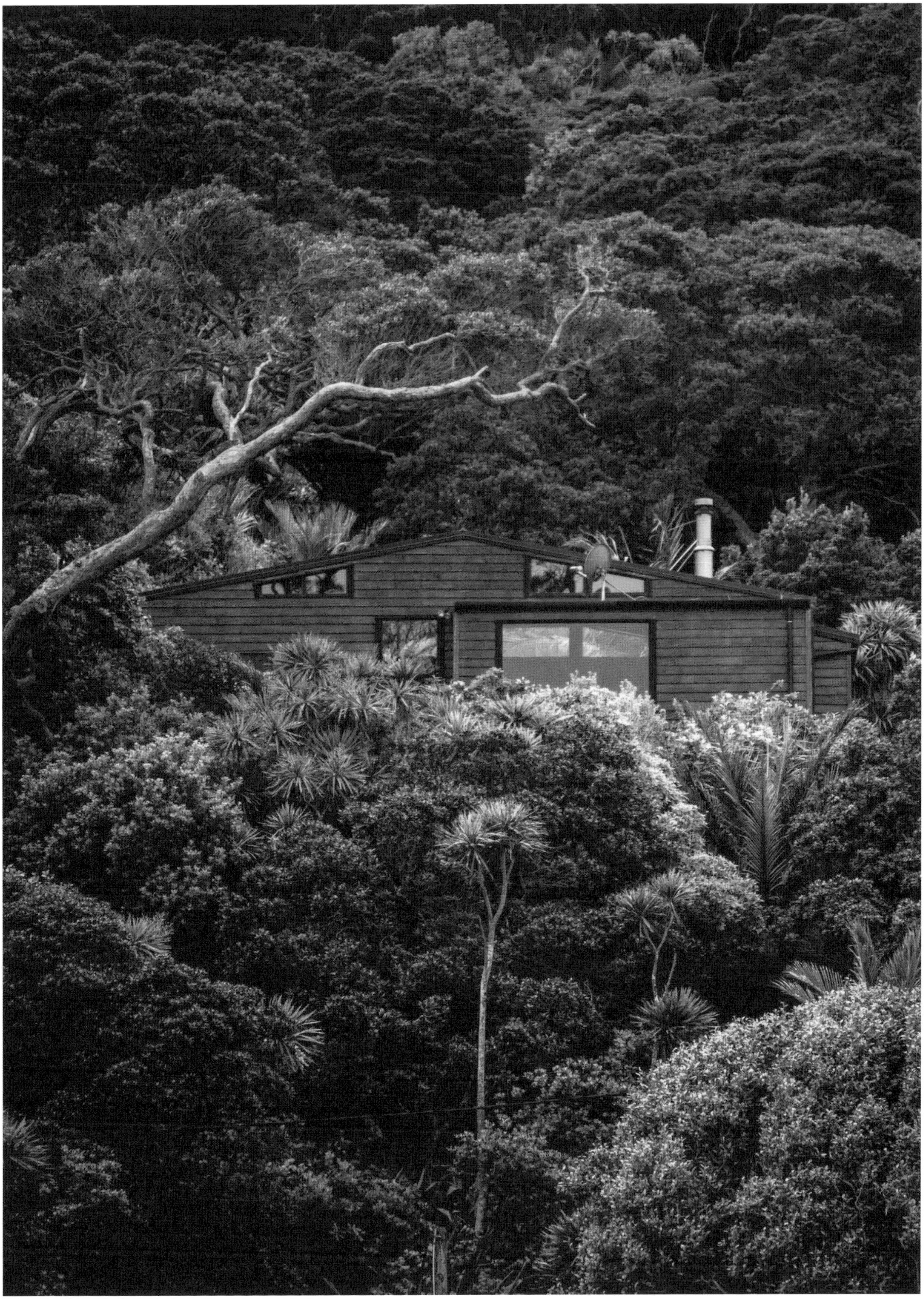

vero
Lumley
TOWER
8900
Alfa Romeo

ZURICH
pwc

EXIT

KAPANUI

205 QUEEN

BRITOMART

AIG
CityLife

Printed in Great Britain
by Amazon

29998724R00025